OF COURSE, THE YELLOW CAB
New and Selected Poems

Ken Champion is a poet, writer, novelist and reviewer whose work has appeared in literary journals in the US and extensively in magazines and anthologies in the UK. He has published two poetry pamphlets, three full collections, a volume of short stories, two novellas and four novels. His work has appeared in literary journals in the US and extensively in magazines and anthologies in the UK. He has worked as a signwriter, commercial artist and, until recently, lectured in sociology for 20 years.

TO: Irena.

Ken Champion

JULY '20.

Also by Ken Champion

Poetry
But Black and White Is Better
Cameo Metro
African Time
Cameo Poly

Fiction
Urban Narratives
Keefie
Noir
Thrust
The Politicos
The Dramaturgical Metaphor
The Beat Years

OF COURSE, THE YELLOW CAB

New and Selected Poems

Ken Champion

The High Window

First published in the UK in 2019 by The High Window Press
3 Grovely Close
Peatmoor
Swindon
SN5 5SN
Email: abbeygatebooks@yahoo.co.uk

The right of Ken Champion to be identified as the author of this
work has been asserted by him in accordance with Copyright,
Designs and Patent Act, 1988.
© Ken Champion 2019
ISBN: 978-0-244-10372-9

Designed and typeset in Palatino Linotype
by The High Window Press.
Printed and bound by Lulu.com.

CONTENTS

Metropoleis

Camera Obscura

Africana

Theatre

Stateside

Lesions

Anthropomorthingy

Retro

Metropoleis

Roma

Over the camouflage cloth south of the Alps
then the sting of sun at Ciampino and the
cab drivers shouting and pushing each other
as they wait for fares that never seem to come.

In the city an old aeroplane droning around with
a *Vota Forza della Libertà* banner fishtailing above
the *Teatro dell'Opera* where the bourgeoisie
clap themselves for being there and the touting
accordionist hissing at his saxophone rival
outside the *Nouveau* feast of O'Brien's bar.

Hearing the scooters through the shuttered window
and glancing at Rafaello's angels on the wall
seeing your questioning eyes as you
gave me a card on which those cherubs
gazed forlornly past me, and now wanting
to send one to you, wishing you were her.

Café E.10

There's a church opposite seen from under the awning
Alice the waitress sits outside with a cigarette
her smoke blowing across the open door
photo of the lunching riveters astride
a New York girder tilting on the wall
bright leaves on the graveyard trees

I hold up a scrawled phonetic of a Romany hello
she frowns, shakes her head, mouths *bunaziua*
the only movement now inside or out,
its owner, legs apart, looks at nothing
a customer stares at his cappuccino froth
the local butcher, grey hair thick at the back,
chin resting on a hand.

And you want to harvest it, bind it,
carry it home, place it on a sill in the sun
sit and look at it all, slowly, considerately;
Alice passes me as I rise from the table
la revedere she says
lahreveedahree I reply…

Krakow Glowny Station

They're round the back, red gash of mouths
black-lined eyes, tops of breasts like white eggs,
their fee chalked on the soles of their shoes

raising a foot to catch trade from passers-by,
commerce scratched away on a pavement
should the police come clumsily grabbing

and there's a girl taller than the others
red stilettos shining in the twilight,
a sudden grin, skips towards a soldier

kitbag dropped at his side, stops for
a second, scuffs her shoe.

The Social Class of Trees

It's their shapes, fan palms, monkey puzzles, the rich
greens, the Highgate Hill of them, fresh leaves hiding
fin de siècle gables, overhanging goggled motorists,
a plaid lapelled entrepreneur, waist-coated Chief Clerk

smiling up through branches, the bright jade light then
downhill east, trees knuckled, dry, council-pollarded,
coalman bending sacks on his shoulder over a doorstep
chute, below, a boy standing on the settling coal, cellar

blurred by dust, running out to a horse pulling a carted
carousel, rides for jam jars, shrimps and winkles from
a barrow. The mother - apple of a street bookie's eye -
a daily herring and bowl of tea seamstress sewing

leg-of-mutton sleeves, lining merry widow hats,
her son playing in a sandpit, looking up; a veranda
glimpsed on the hill, mullioned windows reflecting
the sun, high chimneys, a sunlit, jacketed shoulder
on a camomile lawn, and the splendour'd trees.

Café Slavia

In the painting on the end wall, opposite *Most Leggi* and
the trams, sits a bearded man, head in hands, financial
pages spread, glancing up at a transparent woman, naked,

her arse on the table cloth, arm bent, splayed fingers
taking her weight, foot lightly touching the floor. Her
shoulder's towards him, profile, bobbed hair, quietly

insisting he doesn't have to stay with a spiritually
corseted wife, has only to sweep the papers and his
life onto the parquet and she'll be flesh again, his

hand resting on the inside of her thigh, a chair, baroque
lamp no longer seen through her waist; but it could all
be a businessman's reverie, something to think about

till the waiter arrives bottle in hand, and at the edge
of the picture there he is, foot slightly raised, and
you wonder whether the shoe's going to descend or

rise and whether the girl will disappear as he comes
nearer or if he'll casually ask after *pan's* wife while
looking past him at the Art Deco clock outside.

Hawksmoor Church

It isn't precious, no Catholic gold and glitz,
just white columns, acanthus leaf, rams horns,
dulled oak - a sparrow would look down on grey

heads, black coats, wheelchairs, corner painting
and tomb, hear a violin dirge in a square nave
that's housed hatreds, saccharin cant, that's

never seen a floral *grandad* nor crossed
hammers in claret and blue roses; and this
before the spirit's weakening to the body,

the fidgets, coughs, desire for the wine and
smoked eels, toilets, *Match of the Day...*

Pareidolia

the psychological phenomenon of seeing
meaningful connections in random objects

Staring at the platform wall, Victorian bricks, tiny indents
like the cave-pocked hillside where grandpa George hid
Maria from the *paseos*, thin pointing - Skinny Gwen's legs
hop-scotching between the cracks, smoothness of the
newel post orb, a ball dribbled round a streetlamp,
marbles clacking along the gutter

Fluted up-lights become Corinthian columns, me falling
as the ladder slipped, ticket window's *Art Nouveau* tiles
turn into a city whose boulevard trees are not high
enough to see from the *Sacré-Coeur,* the heels
of a passing woman, like yours, but not scuffed
by the heartbreaking limp

Outside, sky, dove of an evening cloud
silhouetting the hedge when dad died, red plastic
forks in the *Station Café,* the Devil in the detail.

Paseos were executions in the Spanish Civil War.

17

London (1959), Gelatin Silver Print

the back of a city gent fills the left foreground
bowler, newspaper, furled brolly held tightly
man with belted mac, trilby, crosses the road
a long-coated woman on the platform of a bus
heading towards a grainy, grey-fogged St Paul's

       me, skinny teenage apprentice
       lost within newly plastered walls
       I can't prime them I say, too wet
       blow on 'em till they dry says the foreman
       cackles, jeers, brown teeth, fear
       give 'em a coat o' looking at
       shouts Wag, one of the royals
       works lots of weekends, earning,
       they walk away to the caff

silhouette man will not complete his stride
raincoat and hat won't reach the pavement
the woman will never move down the bus.

Street Market, Madrid

Spanish pit bull with painted toes
like a Sumo wrestler wearing lipstick
owner and dog poncing past Pepe's
where she sits bleached and posed

Flicks her long legs
by graffitied *trompe-l'oeil*
nose tilting in disgust at spray can silver
and perspective destroyed
smiles at jazz outside an old *cerveceria*
nods at guitars in an ice-cool bar

Upright down steps
on *Calla Curtidores*
church, verandas, scrolls
Art Nouveau plus God
stops by a stall, the swift choice,
a dress, again it's black.

White Marble Nudes

Stained rocks rise from a pool by the
Thames, atop, two rearing horses,
the chariot between their spread wings
driven by a female, whipless, hair
held high between her fingers,

a maid stretches an arm in worship,
a kneeling nymph helps up a friend,
their arms clasped, another sits in a shell
where, between finger and thumb, a nut
for a horse or pearl for the charioteer.

Arms wide, a girl bends backwards
as if suddenly aware of the animals
above, a lass below leans over the
water, surprised by her reflection, and
as the tide rises, weeds wash up to an
ankle, behind a knee, the palm of a hand.

On the other bank those that look across
may see only a tip of stone above trees,
a curl, a tress, not thinking there could
be figures here larger than life,
elegant, playful, drowning.

Journeys

I've smoothed around Manhattan, slept in Central
Park, seen neon-splattered dawns from the top
of Empire State, strolled Paris streets, climbed
the Spanish Steps in Rome, watched London
villages clone into amorphous mass

what etches the mind is the paint run
on a panelled door, badly cut-in glazing bar,
bright smudge on a tag graffito, a fascia's
pointless apostrophe, not noting countless
chimneys regress to perspective but a single crack

nor seeing your love, compassion, reined-in hurt
but the sliver of gum above front teeth, broken nail
on a little toe, single hair trapped in an earring
the elaborate *l* in *leaving*, undotted *i* in *him* I saw
by chance before you went to post your letter.

War Museum

When the last one's gone they open showcases, put on
uniforms - typists dress as WAAFS - run to the tanks,
unlock caterpillar tracks, slide down cables into the

cockpits of the hanging Heinkel, Spitfire, the one
with the headphones who tears the tickets taps
a dit-dit-dah and the big WW1 Mark 2 turns in

its own length as a jeep with chewing gum colonel
cruises round the hall leaving the battle to a Sopwith
chasing a Focker across the ceiling, silent doodlebug

with caretaker astride, curator and guide in medics'
coats bearing the cleaner away, mop still clenched
in his fist, piercing a tank a shell makes pink spawn

of the archivist as it ricochets for ever until dawn
lights the windows, planes stop circling, medals
return, hair quickly brushed; the first visitor,

the ticket man frowns past him, outside, to the
haze of smoke from the breeches of the 15-inch
naval guns pointing across the Thames.

Freedom Fighter

She walks easily
hijab swirling
in a breezy London park
her gaze straight ahead
on the angry back of a husband

An Islamic possession
she quietly knows
that her cover-up
is as useless as its irony
as her eyes catch mine

and I stop and imagine
dark nipples and smooth legs
as she moves away
female and hidden
in that oppressive black.
And her Nike trainers.

Cities

Screaming subways, clichéd hydrants, grills, steam,
bar-filled Pier 17 serving manhattans to Manhattans
marbled foyers flashy not grand, nor Central
without sunbeams, delis' curled cheesecake
Statue, taking liberties, think of home.

Parks bucolic, stuccoed Chelsea-Ken, magnolia gardens
magic mews, teenage Sloane guiding her horse gently
over cobbles, glint of canal, steepled skylines, chimneys,
Sunday best Africans marching to church, low sun
flooding the Thames, wharves, Canary singing.

Fingerthumbs framing a Georgian window,
director's cut, a thousand pictures never taken,
you, auburn hair an open curtain across your face,
flowing, letting me spread my hands through.

Camera Obscura

Relative Objects

A wall photo of *fin de siècle* Paris like a black and
white Utrillo, winter trees edging the boulevard
narrowing to a fog of branches, a grey pulls a cab,
a man crosses in front, jacket swirling, a fedora'd

poseur stands in the kerb, but it's the foreground
that fascinates; a top-hatted *roué* part-hidden
by a woman's pale face, crinoline hanging under
her coat, their smudged reflections on the wet road,

I wonder if she knows he's there, or the driver,
or *M'sieur* jacket, and if she were to turn to the man
would her perspective be the true one, the best one.
Half way to the counter I drop my cup, the girl

has a broom in her hand before the pieces settle;
to her I'm the man who's dropped a cup, to me
she's the provider of food, to the owner I'm
the one that bids him *gule gule* when leaving

and as I do the cab remains stationary,
it is still cold. I try to imagine
the colour of the woman's eyes.

Gule gule is Turkish for 'goodbye'.

Hidden

The symmetry of Georgian windows
relation of glass to London brick mass
top-heavy chimneys that magic the house
fanlight shapes like dragonfly wings

I finger-frame it, eyes a camera, angle my head
a tree moves across, snout of a stone boar
garden wall hung with forsythia
the door opens, she steps out to go to him

short skirt, glossed lips, mascara eyes
filling the lens and gone - see the house again
note acanthus capitals, ovolo and dart
the portico's Roman swags,
tarted, colonised.

Art Class

She's tall, leather-laced top, lycra leotards,
high boots heeled high, wide cheekbones,
tousled hair, snake tattoo on her arm.

I get her legs okay, the knees, emphasise
painted toes, but it's the face, red fig of a mouth
pixie ears, huge eyes, radiating lashes.

I'm a serious artist, technique, craft, style, but
Reggie captures her exactly, expression, essence,
we huddle round, stare at it, she's standing

astride a stallion circling a ring, whip flicking
the marquee's ceiling, serpents on her shoulder
writhing through her Medusa hair, light flaring

from the animal's hooves till she's all light,
everything's light; but it isn't, it's a crayon sketch
of a slim girl with a shy smile, standing quietly still.

Freezeframe

Bleaklake.
Greydeeped water.
Smudged trainers greensmeared jeans.
Ducks circling their island
under a sky like a shut door.

And me circling you
as you take your colour shots
in glorious black and white
standing scarved and tall
against a background of yourself.

I watch you and wait
your head down fiddling with the camera.
You walk by reeds and I join your step
diffidently edging towards you
as a trail of birds
are trapped in your lens.

And in our sheltering car
we stare through side windows
moving away looking through raindrops
seeing trees standing on their heads,
our worlds in camera obscura.

Deco

The window's large, critalled curves, thin lateral
lines, the branches of an accidental tree in front
touching the glass I look through as if, beyond

were hedges, pantiles, sunray doors, stylised shapes
of shells and aeroplanes, but from the bedroom, over the
leaves, there's a pebble-dashed terrace, latticed panes,

plastic carriage lamps, beer cans flattened in kerbs;
I stride back up the street to finish painting a garden wall
whose owner doesn't know me nor what I'm doing

and move my brush across the render wanting
to push through it, past it, stroke my way back in white
to the *Moderne,* the chevrons, the chrome and black,

not giving a ziggurat for the face
looking through its PVC window.

'Critalled' is a term for steel windows closely associated with the Art Deco
movement.

Trees are Wasted in the Country

They're everywhere,
sprouting from fields, hedges, hills,
tedious canvas of green,
leaves mulching into tractor'd mud,
Disney horror branches against a moon.

In the city they're magic,
a frame for Georgian windows set in London brick,
overhanging park lakes, arching, touching, above an
Edwardian street, bright fans behind Victorian chimneys,
sentries guarding a Palladian villa, a canopy for toppled
tombstones, lightly resting on the head of a Christ,
curled leaves matching a lintel's Art Nouveau scrolling,
emerald waves at the base of a Bauhaus tower,
an Art Deco liner riding a tide.

I'm in a city where you've magicked me; your
garlanded hair, blossomed cheeks, green eyes.
Don't leave. You'd be wasted in the country.

Caffè Ponti

It's hot, boat seats glisten like
lanterns, silver fire reflections
ripple under the bridge, *Si, pasta,*

grins Maria, I sit; on my way
to Dr. Jules, he'll insist again
that *all* creatures fear attack

and lean forward, head pecking,
mimicking fearful eyes, arms
like wings ready for flight,

Hey, she says, *cibo, mangialo!*
You eat like a bird.

It's so hot.

Africana

*You are not a country, Africa. You are
a concept.... a glimpse of the infinite.*

Ali Mazuri

African

slender neck without the rings seen in early sepias,
full lips neither enigmatic nor known,
eyes darker than her lashes
and blacker than the fountained braids
rising above her headband

> and when you mimic me your accent is too strong
> I am Zulu not Afrikaans and when you come
> home with me at Xmas it will be very hot
> but you must wear a suit to show respect
> for my mother and you cannot sleep with me

a languid wisdom inhabits every glance,
every decision, and when music plays
she moves nothing except her wrists,
bending them rhythmically downwards,
casually clutching all the sex in the world

> I am beautiful inside as well as out
> and when I go back I even give them
> my panties because we are poor and if
> I was a virgin you would pay a thousand
> pounds for me and when I was a child
> I walked like an old woman but I am
> holding my shoulders back for you because
> I am glad you took me out though I don't think
> you will come home with me at Xmas

Students, African

Telling them that God was a construct
and that the real question was *why?*
and the classroom glowing
with anger and pity
and me feeling alive.

Telling them about oppression
cloaked in evangelical missions
and childhood sepias
of ringed female necks a foot long
and a *savage* with a bone through his nose.

And the one with
the Stars & Stripes headscarf
whose eyes had drowned
my wine bar seduction
in deep indifference
two nights ago
now telling us the bone
was a fashion statement

and suddenly leaving the room,
with me knowing
that on her mobile
it says *I love Jesus*
and Jesus loves me.

Ashanti

Wisteria hangs from a tea room wall
and a girl in a snooker player's waistcoat
sweeps a table with a cloth
as inside the gate English Heritage
offers a bunch of brochures in return
for five pounds for the House
three for the Grounds

Before settling the chairs the girl turns her head
to glance out at the feather tulips
which could have floated down from parrots
and noting the tribal marks on her cheek
I wonder if she had ever anticipated
serving orange cake at a Tudor palace by the Thames.

Moral Philosophy

Making a *salwar kameez* look utterly African
by wrapping the trousers around her head,
braided extensions pluming above them,
she demands my silence as I suggest
she at last spends a night with me,
yet kneels close with her cheek
on my knee as I correct her work.

Using one hand for the keyboard
I trail the other gently from her ear
to the base of her neck
until she pushes me playfully
to the floor and stands astride me
her eyes black and still.

But it's church day and at any time
she can say, as she does, she has to go
and holding her folder walks to the gate
while I return to the screen
where her essay title still reads:
'Thou shall lie only with whom thou love.'
Old proverb. Discuss.

First Day Back

Despite their stifled yawns
he tries to tell them about Marx
and sum up his thesis in a sentence.
Our reality, consciousness, identity,
our political, cultural and economic systems
are determined by the ways in which we
technologically transmute the physical world.
What do you think then? he asks. Is it true?
You've got ten seconds to answer.

They look alarmed, so he holds
his hands out, fingers cupping,
encouraging. *Joke*, he says, *joke.*
You'd prefer a story, wouldn't you?
and their grins explode. *Yes*, they shout,
like sitting round a fire telling tales.
He could see firelight flickering on their faces.

They're smiling now; tall, smooth-skinned
Somalians, gaunt Rwandans, gentle
full-faced Ghanaians, gold bangled
Nigerians making their Victorian values heard
(not for them the two inch band of flesh
at their waist, tops of knickers showing)
and the two Dagenham lads, sitting apart,
asking if this geezer was a brother of Groucho.

He sighs, smiles back at them,
asks how their summer had been.

Atheist at River of Life Pentecostal

Driving with Tapo, twelve, and he knows the short cuts,
industrial streets, factories, dishevelled gym, and there are
the signs, neon strips, day-glo - churches competing for
God, Thandi whispers - and on the ground floor there's

Living Gospel Of Christ, two hundred arms rising, go to the
next floor, tell Tapo I got lost, Jesus will find you, he says,
smaller space, preacher in cream-coloured dress, *okome aka
bababa,* a seven year old in a pin-stripe pacing in the audience,

eyes ordering us to pray, year-old Emmanuel jumping up and
down on his chair to the music, singer soft-shoe shuffling across
the stage, Tapo playing drums, the girl in the corner, high cheek-
bones, an Acholi Beyonce, spread fingers turning into rhythmic

fists, the pastor suddenly here, large man, messianic, bass
voice rising, *You must fear the Lord* he glowers at me, then
softer, sensing a convert, *Christ is waiting, let him in;* just a
quiet keyboard now, Thandi kneeling, *Hallelujah, Hallelujah,*

and as Tapo guides us back I smile smugly, knowing that
after the tea and biscuits I beat the pastor at ping-pong.

Girl, African

She walks in with a parcel
of stuffed fish-heads and yams
and begins washing up while they warm
and casually sucks one of the eyes
while I open the wine and watch her
take off the trainers that make her limp.

Her smile pretends to like my music
and there's the usual bedroom struggle
to remove her clothes
until she clamps my wrist
and I notice the rag around her waist
which, she has said, she wears for fasting
and she still hasn't spoken a word.

I remind her that last month
it was the blood that had stopped her
because it was against her beliefs
and now it's *more* religion, and will it,
I ask, be a headache next time.

She dresses swiftly,
her Nefertiti head upright and still,
and with a flat-vowelled finality
suggests I write a poem about it,
and soundlessly leaves the house.

Theatre

Funny Girl

In charge, young as I was, of refurbishing
Streisand's dressing room for her six-week
stint as Fanny Bryce and working hard
for time to sit, overalled, at the back
of the stalls to watch rehearsals and
her complaining that her lunch box
was too heavy to hold.

The shouts for a new one
from director and cast echo away
in diminishing regress as her Bronx
impatience clears the stage, then suddenly
the soaring perfection of *People,*
the silence, the unscripted applause
including ours, as she finishes
professional and deadpan.

And her next song crushed short
by a demand from the circle
for the conductor to get it right
and he, like a nervous butterfly
claiming he was following the score
and the theatre filled with the rasp of
'I *wrote* the fuckin' score!'
On the way home the Standard's headline
of 'Jule Styne Sacks British Conductor'
does not carry the crassness,
nor the beauty.

Usherettes

Some serve in a churchlike Athens Odeon, an act of observance
and Greek dubbing, others in Sao Paulo's Una Banco pimping
ice cream while waiters tout margaritas, a Tangier picture
palace where the audience shouts *look behind you!* to the hero,
comfort refugees in a shell-pocked art house in Beirut, watch
contraband movies in an Art Deco theater amongst Havana
palms, fight off the manager of the Roxy in Taiwan.

They've heard the roar of light hit the screen, ping of a bra
strap from the back row, watched a lit match passed like
an Olympic flame across red velour seats, cigarette smoke
floating into bas-reliefs and chevrons; torch beams gliding
over carpets they are ciphers guiding us into the city,
its mansions, bedrooms and bars.

There's one now, next to my aisle seat, raised knee flicking
off a shoe, leaning back on the curtained wall, unlit torch
idly hanging, the world at 24 frames a second in her eyes.

Pedestal

In a Barcelona street there are statues that aren't real
they're people standing still
till the chink of coin elicits an arrogant turn of head
from a marble-veined Columbus
or a smirking salute from a copper cast G.I.

And there's a bronzed centurion who raises his spear
and a golden pair of potentates who bow
as pesetas rattle their boxes
whilst a man made from chalk with a guitar and a scowl
merely plucks a string as a grinning tourist drops a cent.

But it was the girl made from lead
with an errant wisp of hair, spinning her
grey rose and blowing slow kisses
who entranced me into daylong gazes
at her Eliza Dolittle face and small sweet waist.

I brought her home a month ago
but it's too cold to play statues so she dresses up
and stands in front of our mirror perfectly still for hours
until I come home and place a penny in her little box
when she twirls her drab rose and pouts her lips.

And when in bed I touch her leaded hand
she shrugs and murmurs in that Catalan way
I'm tired, I've been on my feet all day.

Afternoon Movie

You go in knowing it's already started;
there's a close-up of a girl staring across
a stretch of water, profile, tear on her cheek -
this time you don't look for the camera's
reflection - then the static shot, full face

looking sad as she drives along a road,
not even the upward, arcing angle of tree tops
to lessen the intensity, and you wonder what's
happened to her, a father dying, a crushed child,
and you know that soon the scene will end,

she'll get out, technicians take the camera
off the bonnet, unit director smiles and brushes
her cheek as the chief grip laughingly drives the
car away, she'll light a cigarette, yawn, tell
a stunt man jokingly to piss off; all the time

that first shot of her is flooding your mind,
and you want to be with her, just with her,
looking across the water.

Cotton Documentary Short: Visuals

titles, intro and music agreed, commentary under discussion
long-shot London Bridge, morning rush hour; slow zoom
to walkers clothes: shirts, jackets, trousers; dolly up to grey
sky, merge into blue; lock down on white-tinted landscape;
mid-shot of head-scarved women filling baskets, grinning
to camera through mist of candy floss cotton; pan right
to plantation owner's beaming face, arms paternally spread
shots of females showing bruises from overseers' sticks redundant

cut to rolling lorries, drivers' thumbs-up from cab windows
to roadside camera; close-up of auctioneer's hammer; shot
of clapping bidders; mid-shot of looms, shaking, sifting haze
becoming thread; cut to rollers pressing out cloth; long-shot
of goods trains silhouetted against a tropical sun
grip's snaps of 24 hour-shift drivers asleep at wheel not needed

aerial long-shot (drone) of slowly turning container ship;
upward arc of dockside gantry swinging container onto
truck; fade to exterior of shining new factory - CGI - trucks
unloading; cut to interior, young women, hair in buns,
chatting at machines; close-shot of spread fingers
positioning pockets, hems, labels; fade to reverse zoom
of opening shot, but with sunny sky
closing credits as agreed
gaffer's pics of needle-pierced fingers
and footage of smiling soldiers at gates pretending to shoot him unwanted

Nike interested in product placement

Festival

Watching last rehearsals in the old market,
rising klaxon of trumpets and drums
then collecting the canes to bind borders
round the crowds in the park near the zoo.

In they come, symphony everywhere,
clarinets, saxophones, trombones, flutes
the two trumpets behind a tree
one turning a second before the other
taking the pitch perfectly,
for a while the silver sax on the café roof
your blazed hair, lips smiling around the mouthpiece,
fluttering hands for the scribble
one two three four, arms flung, *cut*.

Crowd thinning, I pick up flattened sticks
muddied string, help pack instruments, reflected glory.
They go to the pub still in *this beautiful world* T-shirts
high fives, talking tunes, percussion discussion,
me trailing a bundle of bamboos
like a mate-less panda.

Locations

I find the places for shooting scripts: mean streets with
terraced houses built straight from pavements, nestling
Cotswold cottages, an Essex windmill, a Hertfordshire

mansion without a games room and footballer's pool.
I skip-read contexts; it's a sci-fi says the director
but I like these Bermondsey back alleys, this one's

in the East End, but I'm enraptured with a Georgian
square in Chelsea, Regency houses in Sussex, I'm
told it's a period piece when I've just fallen for the
curved diamonds of the gherkin.

Perhaps it was the same with you; you asked for love,
I gave counterfeit smiles, my time, bought you a watch,
you wanted to care for me, I enjoyed my carelessness.

But I'm going to change; be the man that spins the
wheel on the overturned car at the end of the film.

Genre: Gangster

i.

close shot, lipstick-glistened,
mascara'd, leans forward,
rucked stocking over toes,
unrolling, whispering, shining

ii.

flat road across wheat fields,
mid-shot following a Buick,
fedora'd silhouette, hidden
briefly by a farmhouse,
beyond the dusty yellow
rises Chicago, its towers pushing
into the pale air, curved back
of the car moving towards it

iii.

street lamp, a girl passes, turns into
an alley, cars swishing, receding,
camera gliding through a doorway,
moves jerkily up stairs, two men
struggle in a room, one crashes through
a window, the sound loud, sharp

the body sprawled on cobbles,
faint saxophone as if played streets
away, cut back to the room, tall man,
side of his face lit in the dimness,
We did it, Tilly, he's gone

down again, she's glancing up
from the alley straight at the lens,
smiling, turns, stilettos fading,
saxophone swelling

iv.

a *Pathe* newsreel of a scene
corpse in monochrome
white shirt, black trousers
dark blood drying on the head,
a woman stares at a gun, loose in her hand,
curve of the handle, colour, texture,
frowns in three-quarter profile, blurs,
a rising shoe sharply focused as the door
closes behind, she sits, leans forward,
picks up a stocking.

Brief Encounters

The brown carriages, waiting room,
porters, pistons, steam, the refreshment
room tea urn, hat stand, trilbies, fox furs,

the woman, respectable, pain in her eyes,
brave mouth, walking along a platform
towards the camera and away from her

almost-lover; the screen in the darkness,
front seats, aisles, usherettes at the back,
torches still, recognising the stifling duty

of their own Saturday night giving - bearing
the weight, smelling the Woodbines and ale -
and watching her straight back, shoulder pads,

wanting her to turn and run back to him, leap
through the smoke, rise above the sooted
columns, shatter the roof, soar…

Random Spanish Lesson

Half way up the stairs to the launch, the toilet,
stench, turbo drier, a speaker in the ceiling:
'Say English.'
'Ingles.'
'Do you understand? '
'¿Entiendes? '
'I do not understand.'
'No entiendo.'
'Do you speak Spanish?'
'¿Hablas Español?

In the room, a malice of poets, swirl of pearls
and jeans, a weariness of *shards* and *souls,*
adjectival gluts, neo-surrealists dwelling
up their arses, and the high voice rising
at the end of each line:
'We see Rokohiv after Samothrace,
Free of Pisistratus,
Oh! bright Apollo…'

Down the stairs again,
the half open door,
'No entiendo.'
'No entiendo nada.'

Stateside

Of Course, the Yellow Cab

It's forty nine fifty, you wan' I give back the fifty cents?
and passing Jimmy's Bar with screens showing baseball
silhouetting its clients, Speedy's deliquintescence for
brunch, eggs over, rye, easy on the cheese, subway to
Brooklyn *You shoulda taken the A train.*

Coffee at Juniors, bow tie waiters, photos of Rita,
Gable, Flynn - it's eighty and humid, Chrysler glistens,
walk over the bridge, see Liotta in back of an NYPD car
Brando toughing it on Pier 17, New Jersey accent
of a Cagney cop, Hackman still and tense on Line 4
Grand Central and sunbeams.

Sailors in threes on the town in Times Square
neon-edged night from the top of the Empire
think of the captain crooning *Your small town blues*
they're melting away as we came in to JFK,
the sting of tears, stare at the sidewalk,
cabs pass me by.

Girder Men Photo

It's as if they're in the bleachers waiting for
a game to start, the one on the end cadging
a light from his buddy, another peeking at
a workmate's lunch, the cloth caps, boots,
East River beyond, Manhattan below.

Tomorrow the man at the side of the cable
is playing pool with Ed and the boys downtown,
the hatless one's with his dark-haired Sue
at Coney Island, elbows jutting in contrapposto
burlesque giggling into a Kodak, the man with
the vest and the take-my-wife jokes *she's so fat*
wherever she sits she's always next to me drinks
at a bar in Hoboken, the rest of them in a theater
on Times Square, fight at Madison, a diner.

Then it's back to the metal, chains, the rivets,
the heaving, pushing, the grappling with
memories they can't hold, which float away,
snatched by the high wind below the steel.

Auction, Memphis

Two dollar bill two dollar bill da-labil da-labil da-labil

you wanna bid that fifty cent crate Larry? we got
some pillers and sheets here Bentwood rocker
blue crock bowl and Bob stop strokin' that dress
she's gone now and ah put it there anyways
and yeh I shoulda gotten more fer yer house and
tractor too and Josh that woman o' yours
sure got a sparkle in her eyes these days, well she
has when she looks at me, boy, and Tom, livin' on
yer own now uh? well I got at least two, might
let yer share one, ha ha, and best keep yer womenfolk
at home next week those of yer still got 'em, it's mah
diamond-studded belt they lerv, and don't forget
we're over at Ray Bang's gun store then and ah might
just have a mind to let yer bid for pieces o' yer lives back

Two dollar bill two dollar bill da-labil da-labil da-labil...

Dad's Grub

We walk Brooklyn Bridge, touring, laughing,
try a Bronx accent for their old East End ritual
waddya wan' Alf, two cheese, one o' jam, uh?
doin' a double shift tonite Edie, gimme a slice
o' bread and drip and a tomayta.

We're heading Downtown, but I see us all at
Clacton, knotted hanky on his head, paddling,
squinting at the sand, roll-up dangling from
his lip, mum square-jawed in a deckchair.

In front now, bruv's mimic of *that soddin' boy*
stops the laughter, it's still inside us: the brass
stair rods, silent meals, bent knife trapping the
gravy, *workin' it up, an' I,* the tassled table cloth,
echo of a key in the cheaply grained door, the
grim mat-stamping, shaking of a wet raglan.

He lets me catch up, turns his head, smiles,
silently mouths *Bleedin' Yanks,* we stride on,
the *Eastside Deli* straight ahead…

Chicago, Descending

The fanned ochre stripes across glistening grey sheets
is uninhabited land, the snowdrifts outside the window
are strata-cumulus two miles below, and that's not

a white-beach bay, but a reservoir with suds
around its edges, while the green inked sponges
and pop-up houses are an infinite suburbia.

Here, off the Loop, the Franklin Center's Art Deco
fools, as does Union Station's ticket hall, its
black and silver fountain a nineties mock.

And in a motel on LaSalle, your construct
of a smile, a deceit.

Model Soldiers

Wearing camouflage suits
matching tank tops and desert boots
Sam Brown belts
leather holster accessories

mandatory shades and optional berets
razor-edged flat to the sides
of Clooney stubbled faces
with grey cropped hair

rogering the rear of Havanas
with matches before suckling,
here they come. Mom's apple pie
colonels catwalking across the world.

Lesions

Finger

In the photo the beach, distant *Kursaal*, little brother and
dad smiling at each other, me, lank teenage hair, sulking;
it's still there, the complete finger, the whole nail, my hand

on a gabardined knee, and hours later I drag a deckchair
across, playfully kicked away by Tommy as I clutch under-
neath, my weight taking the flesh, splitting the bone, splayed

like a cut radish, stare at the spinning sand as if I could find
the top somehow; look at it now, shortened, the underside
a slight cleft, as if time lay in it; but it's a finger, it's done

things, touched, pushed, cursed, gripped, trailed from your
shoulder, your arm, hand, let go, its numbness in acres of
air as I wait for you to return, to put it back, the tip.

An Interest in Architecture

I always look up to spot the good bits: the odd
castellations on top of an Edwardian hotel, the white
pediment above high Victorian keystones, the set-back
top of a thirties block like the bridge of a liner sailing
out of an Art Deco poster.

Walk steadily, a straight line, even paced, disturbing
no-one, yet people stride across me, force me to halt,
look down, frown, I flick my shoe, catch their heel,
they stumble, glare, as I shrug, raise eyebrows,
feign apology, smile.

There's been an accident outside the church, ambulance,
police, blue cordon siphoning traffic, a stretcher, oxygen
mask, splint, broken shoe, all that's seen through a rush
of paramedics, people lean on barriers, part of them
wanting to watch death.

A woman runs in front of me, laughing, knocking
my arm, trips as my foot snakes out and I catch for an
instance the black eyes, blind to me upon the road,
and she isn't laughing but wailing *No No No*
as a policeman runs to her,

guides her to a car, pushes her head under the rim of the
door arch, and the dreadful stare trying to see the figure
in the street under tight grey blankets, turn my back,
glance up at a Catholic Jesus, the gash of colour on the
lips, like the slice of red on the roadside tuft of hair.

Osteopath

A lively laugh would push through to the waiting room,
proud voice talking endlessly of his son's trial for
Spurs, hinted at by the school team photo that's no

longer on the wall, just a clout nail and a rectangular
line of dust, and the silence. He shakes hands, thumb
and finger on my hip, *the leg's long, sacra-iliac,* I lie

back, my arms in the crux of his, pulls me up, around;
in his head he's lifting a child onto his shoulders, podgy
legs round his face, and releasing me, the boy helpless

with laughter falls across his bed in the mock fight,
kneading my neck he turns my head and sees wide
eyes playing hide and seek, gripping my calf the lad

slides into a tackle, flying up the stairs as fingers
climb my spine, ruffling the boy's hair as his hands
dig deeper into the back of my skull.

Cafe

The sweet froth gulp of cappuccino, it's baby, breast,
silent suckling in a tender universe, *Jo reggelt!* from
the waitress like a mother smiling, I lean back, lying

in a cot again, pavement plane trees like a canopy,
suddenly the smell of sauce on hot chips, inimical,
attacking, remember dad's fists, the slit eyes, brown

teeth, the hands smashing down, fork spinning
from a plate, arcing into a wall, see him outside
a pub, the vinegar'd cockles, flexing his calves

as if ordering another pint, canines ripping
a whelk; the waitress asks if I'm okay,
I nod, leave, the trees dripping ketchup.

Jo reggelt is Hungarian for 'good morning'.

Cannonball

I'd go in after the clowns, he says, before
the finale with the Cossacks - as cockney as
I am - riding round the outside of the ring.

Giovanni would crack his whip
point to the big gun being pulled in and
roar, *The loneliest place in the world!*

They're in the park, he's sitting with them, bog-eyed kids.
There'd be a roll of drums, he whispers, and I'd strut to it
dressed all in white, turn to the crowd, bow, climb in,

'course, it had to be pointed at the right angle
too low and I'd have missed the net, too high
and I'd have weighed thirty stone when I hit it.

He stops, slowly turns his head, scanning them,
they haven't moved an eyelid. He adjusts his
blanket, flicks the brake, wheels himself away.

Philosophy

Think vaguely as you shut your door
of quantum's idea that infinity reverts to nothing

and wonder whether a nought is mere coincidence
or states the ultimate tautology, and as I walk away

realise your never-ending love has turned to zero,
the shape of your lips as you told me to go.

Tube

The eyes in the solipsistic mirror, the widening gaze
to brush the lashes, mascara, underlining, narrowing
for the rouge, the lipstick gloss, glimpse of bleached

teeth, comb tweaking a fringe, the unbuttoning, bra
dropped on the next seat, the bared breast, practised
pencil dotting underneath, Stanley knife making an

arced incision, the jelly-like mould pushed into the
cut by her palm, threaded needle, sutures, scissors
to finish; the other breast, the gentle fastening, deftly

gathered tools, mirror, the copy of *Hello!* walks out
the opening doors; I look at the floor, the forgotten
knife, want to rush it to her for the cut behind the ear,

the tucked skin, a scarf to hide the bruise, but stare
at the rolling lipstick half risen from its holder,
splash of blood, a tear.

Surrogate

He's found a mannikin that was skipped
on one of his walks where he stares at dogs,
it's male, but it'll do, can't afford a blow-up.

He's in the shed with it, shadows from neighbours
gardens are curling over the fence trying to look in,
it's lying there like a Christ, he folds its arms down.

He has an old bra, ties it round its chest,
paints the scuff on the leg with *Hint of Peach*
washes the brush, spins it dry, a craftsman.

Peers through a cobwebbed window,
getting dark, switches on the light,
marks a line between the thighs.

Wittgenstein

Why did people think that the sun went round the earth
he asked. Because it looked as if it did I said.
But, what would it look like if it *looked* as if the earth

went round the sun? It does I said, thus it would look
the same. As if the sun goes round the earth then? Yes.
You haven't answered my question he said, smiling.

Think about it he grinned, walking away, voice trailing.
He wanted me to ponder tautologies, infinite regress
the way the world appears, our perceptions of it.

All I could think of was what it would look like
if it *looked* as if you loved me.

Things

Gaps in wardrobes
spaces in cupboards
he knows she's gone
but ornaments remain;
Wedgwood, Lladro figurines
Regency beaux, flower sellers
a girl with a cake teasing a dog
two children in a nursery fight
one holding a pillow above her head
like a murderous leg of lamb.

He places them on the floor
a sheep standing in a saucer
an owl upside down in a bowl
lovers in an armless embrace
the new stumps strangely aged
gathers handfuls, armfuls, sackfuls
lays them in a line in the hall
treads on the protruding spout
of an elephant teapot.

Love I Guess

This morning
you were a mother shouting at a child
your fear-born anger pinning me to the wall
mouth open (dummy's imprint still moist)
my flattened hands spanned wide
and my man's body stilled
as my direct gaze pretended to look at you.

But now at night
as I ease from you
to trudge to the bathroom
your arms move a fraction too late
to cling to me
and you hold yourself and whimper.

I wish I could turn back clocks
and lend you my thumb.

Marx in The Park

He bumps into a bench, jumble of books, papers
under his arms, sits beard on belly, stares at a tree,
found himself in Starbucks an hour ago looking across
to a golden M, people dressed oddly, shouting at things
held to their ears, giving strange money to bargirls,
bitte, wievel kostet, proszę , familiar accents, looks
at a book, frowns, shakes his head, it's the translation,
No, he didn't say that, picks up a newspaper, stares
in disbelief at page three, on four a picture of Bush
on his first visit to Asia and somewhere before
Gazza 'Aza Dazzler two lines that say India
gets a McDonalds - did he not say the state is but
a committee for managing the affairs of the bourgeoisie?

Thinks back to his coffee, gazing out the window,
vehicles flashing past posters *my ipod my music
my life* smiles, lips shape the words *technological
determinism,* looks up, pink-clad chavs all around him,
aggressive blind eyes, tight pony tails, point at him,
loser, they chant, *loser, fuckin' loser.*

Timeshrink

She walks into the bar
but it's eight years and the
spitting eyes are quieter,
fragmented soul seems gently whole
and long legs now stretch her jeans.

She talks of her mother, brother, things.
I listen, practised half-smile,
raised eyebrow, quizzical glance
trowelling maturity all over her
as I ask the bouncer
to turn the music down.

She gives me a lift and as we stop
I mention the million memories
we haven't mentioned
and getting out remember to ask
what she's doing these days.
I'm a therapist now she says.

As she drives away
her hair is fair and long again
waist sweet and small
and the night is dense, dark,
hard, like a wall.

Shut

There's a cycle outside the station, not
with the others, but on its own, against
a lamp post, shop lights silhouetting it,

we keep looking at it, the saddle, tyres, the clamp,
she says she's lost the key, everything seems locked,
buildings, buses, cars, the beer can in the fist of

a man sprawled beneath a wall, a statue, the sky,
we step back, still examining its details, stillness,
lack of movement; note her fair hair, pinched lips,

catch each other's eyes, look away
feeling as useless as death.

Dad

He flings my book at the living room wall
with a hollering *You're always fuckin' reading*
me wondering with schizoid irrelevance what
page it would land at, stare at the butler sink,

tin bath on the fence by the toilet. Settles on his
chair looking like a rabbit eating cabbage, bends
his knife to harvest the gravy, lips tighten,
swallows, leans back, wavy hair, tiny eyes that

look surprised when a joke is explained, East Ender,
always buys a round *You're as good as Charlie* prods
mum. Takes me to Brick Lane, smug smiles when
he grabs a bargain, endless *guvs* to the landlord,

postman, everyone, explosive fist once denting our
biscuit tin, photos of army days in India, tells me to
Get a trade in yer 'ands; I start an apprenticeship he
never sees me finish, and yesterday, clearing out

my life before I move, find the same volume,
dog-eared, torn, and in the early morning mist
by his grave, place it carefully on the wet grass
like a book of remembrance.

Anthropomorthingy

Carpet

Bully boy cousin says it's twelve by ten
and though he doesn't want it
I still have to pay him
and we drag it from his loft
down the stairs through the door.

I timidly suggest it's too big
so he rolls it across the road
demanding the size of my room
razor knife clenched and poised.

He stands as he did when we were six
and I could smell the putty on his hands
as he chopped and shaped a little house
pulling the roof off, pushing it into my face.

A car glides round the corner
and neatly bisects us as we step back.
It's okay I say, it's perfect.
The tyre marks exactly match
the chevrons on my Art Deco tea set.

Partytime

In her flat they ask me what I do
I tell them I provide the lulls
in conversations at parties
and after Maria pushes through the crowd
outside *El Español* wailing that nobody loves her
the waiter, familiar, gives us a table for ten.

Carla leans across and gives me *It Ain't Necessarily So*
but won't do *Fever* because she hasn't sung since Italy
you will now I slur bravado as birthday girl Jocasta
hands me paella with a rigid hand
and Moldo the Finn mimics my London glottal
taking our pictures endlessly on his mobile
and making me promise to get drunk with him.

I tell them to give me any girl's name
and I'll know a song about her
and when someone says Dumaci
sing *Happy birthday dear Dumaci*
and shout *¿dónde está la parada por favour?*
knowing as Carla blows me a kiss
and I push a twenty under Jocasta's plate
she won't ask me back next year.

Rewind

At dawn I draw the curtains and roll into bed
where I dream till the previous evening
of old trains sucking smoke from the sky
and stopping when the man
lowers his green flag.

During the day my shaver
plants bristles in my chin
and my teeth produce foam
which I remove perfectly with a brush
after backcombing my hair into disarray.

Looking at where I've come from
I ease into a classroom
where students ask answers
before I give questions
and make notes before I speak.

And I feel the pain before I see you
silently pass along the corridor
and remember that soon
I will bump out of you again.

Anthropomorthingy

I once read a poem written by a wall
and how the squeezed mortar felt.
And one from a pond telling how
it was when a child drowned in it,
His mother churning my depths
with his name. And verses
by a hyena. I'm not laughing,
a hyena, *I trot, I lope, I slaver.*

I'd like to write one about being
a tortoise and what it's like
to have hares gallop past
and the triumph of just beating one
that started three days earlier.

Or perhaps some stanzas
from the Woolwich ferry
as it diesels across grey water
and dreams of gliding into Rio.

I'm not going to though.
It's silly.
And anyway I can't.
I'm a sideboard.

Double Agent

Made a pass at the quarry early on.
Background OK, the right school, said sources.
Informal exchanges; my second-rate intellectualism
her perfect profile and me dangling bits of Marx.
Come up and see my ideologies
let me remove that flimsy materialism
from your shoulders.
Pull our cover over us.

Became your controller, handled you well.
Taught you tradecraft. Becomes a habit
like placing carefully over locks
a strand of your chestnut hair
a thread of cotton from your blouse over hinges
leaving honest dust untouched on your prised open desk
and using shop window reflections
to watch you watching me watching you.

Tried resisting suspicion
(never resealed your envelopes *too* perfectly)
but the smudged arrows chalked on walls
ceased piercing hearts and began pointing nowhere
and our dead letterboxes started dying.
I saw your desire for democracy
the dagger under your cloak
eyes begging me to close your file.

Interview

I told him I was late because
when I woke this morning
everything in my apartment
had been stolen and replaced
with exact replicas.

He asked me what skills I had
I told him I did *very* abstract paintings
no paint, brushes or canvas
but I did buy some second-hand paint
in the shape of a house.

I told him I got on with colleagues
I'd just asked the typist out
but she said if I had sex with her
and she found out I'd be in trouble.

He asked me if I was married
I told him I was divorced
we'd split the house fifty-fifty
she got the inside.

He asked me lots of questions.
I didn't get the job.

Shoulderhouse

You wanted to move your furniture in you said,
all your goods and chattels
into the slope of my shoulder
- which perfectly fitted your head
and where I ran through your hair with bitten nails,
you wanted to live there permanently
your forehead on my cheek.
You would line up your pots on my collarbone
and, slim and gawky, use your utensils
to cook things, nourishing, satisfying my bland tastes,
clean the kitchen with baby oil rubbed into my neck,
relax with sighs to watch the videos in my eyes.

You hung out the washing on the line of my jaw,
completed a jigsaw puzzle of my profile,
bathed nightly in my clavicle's hollow
and brushed your hair with the curls on my chest.
But you no longer live in my shoulder,
you have moved out, stripped it bare
and now dwell in your own being
where I follow you around looking for myself
as you grow tall and strong
from sucking the marrow of my soul.

Mindset

I'm a manic depressive.
I hate everything.
I go around with tins of emulsion
dabbing over un-needed apostrophes
and tour cafes to inform their owners
that 'bolognese' doesn't have an 'a'.

I hate estuary drawl, Big Brother,
people with perfect teeth
and aged skins wearing Arsenal shirts,
as well as middle class inarticulates who say
you know three times in one sentence
and footballers who say *obviously*
when it obviously isn't.

I hate never knowing
where the beans are in Tesco's.
I hate white goods, brown goods,
goods trains, good times.
I hate kids who call me *mister*.
I hate kids.

And I hate women like you,
who find themselves and then
find they no longer love me.
And I *hate* manic depressives.

Brian

He always comes late so as not to help move the desks,
we've got the room ready, new model tonight, black,
seems ordinary, flowered dress, velvet hat, flat shoes,

she strips behind the curtain, enters, lies on a duvet,
a glistening athlete, frizzy hair part hidden by curled
fingers, silver nails, the curve of her back, African arse,

everything; lines, angles, roundness, her shoulders,
breasts, an insane perfection, I try charcoal, pen, acrylic
- she doesn't move - crayon, biro, chalk, tape more paper

to the easel, she sits up, smiles, I look away, she rests
on her back, I settle for a 4B, scratch, shade, rub a curve
with a finger till the paper's worn through; she dresses,

signs for her fee, leaves, he sneaks out with her,
so as not to help with the desks.

Doubt

Never been *really* sure.
Had some clues though:
a male model glimpsed in an art class
long-legged Eurasian youths
curly haired teenaged twins
their tight jeans prettyboying them along
their provocative pavement
and, once, the flash of a scaffolder's buttock.

But then, there was the girl I watched
walk gloriously out of Women's Studies
tossing an auburn mane in derision.
And the women who don't quite
cross their legs on underground trains.
Even the sepia thrill of a Victorian nude.

I've heard that when two people are
attracted to each other at a party
the man may rhythmically skim a finger
round the rim of his wine glass
whilst the female gently massages
the stem of hers between fingers and thumb.

And here at the end-of-term do
I sip my drink and am entranced
by the lilting profiles
of the Principal's daughter
and the slim man from Admin
leaning against the wall.

Oops!

Butterfingers.

Technician

He sits there surrounded by dentures,
ivory white molars, incisors, plaster casts,
I watch him through his window, smoothing

pink plastic, chrome plates, gentle scuffings,
rubbings, levelling a palatal extrusion, notice
when he burrs down a canine he grinds his own

right or left depending what side of a set he's
working on, stops when a girl walks into the room,
breast pressing against her white smock, callipers

in hand, he grins, squeezes her buttocks as she turns
away, then next to me a woman frowning at him,
wedded familiarity oozing through the glass,

he smiles silent words to her, lying through his teeth.

Greenfingers

The fern you brought me
before you left
is now cascading
over the table.
I watch it. Withering.

The yucca in the corner
turns away embarrassed
hiding its leaves
against the wall
pretending not to notice.

The mantelshelf ivy
creeps towards
the TV seeking
escapist entertainment
and trying not to say
I told you so.

Swaying slowly
the spider plant
waits to devour me.
But like you it
probably won't bother.

Retro

50s Noir

It's the lighting; a beach hut's sculpted shadows,
a white face pushing from a darkened porch,
Mitchum in Acapulco heat, slatted light

across his jacket, Greer walking in against the sun,
a Mexican Dietrich strolling a highway, headlights
stroking her back before she becomes night,

the palms, fedoras, wise guys, bars;
the evening park, a tram's *Nighthawks* figure,
kids playing floodlit footie around a lamppost,

the hall glow through the fanlight, lincrusta,
dad's torch searching the cellar for the nail jar,
Aunt Flo upstairs hoping I'll pencil a seam

down the back of her painted legs while
Uncle Harry's away, her face under mine,
garish, by the cheap bedside lamp.

A pencilled line simulated real stockings.

Conservation Area

The pavement trees weren't there then, nor the
leaded glass in the Brown's cricket-balled fanlight
and the rugby pitch in place of the sandpit, swings,

the see-saw escape from god-fearing Gothic that pressed
us all flat, booted, open collars over sports jackets, and
high-skirted Jeannie dancing past Fat Freddy's to the

sweet shop, footballer-owned *Alma Arms, Dellamura's*
ice cream, public baths, Nobbsy and me smashing
a window, ripped hand still scarred, nor the slatted

blinds, matt front doors, the awninged Latvian deli
comfortable as a Paris street corner, but the City
Corporation sign at the park entrance proudly black

in the sun remains, with the genitals I chiselled on its
edge when I was ten.

Period Piece

They're looking at a house, arguing whether
it's Victorian or Edwardian - one points out the
former's yellow stocks, slate roof, cannon head
chimneys, the other, the latter's multi-paned sashes,
veranda, fish scale hanging tiles

as if there is a moment when a house must change
from one style to another, that the foreman, learning
of a Queen's death, would carry on helping a mason
lift a gargoyle, tell labourers to continue mixing
cement or shout for them to cease

a carpenter to lay down his saw, bricklayers their
trowels, carry them home, bossing mallets, hammers,
ask them to wait till a decision be made, perhaps
to start again, the blueprints, young architect,
cravatted, elegant, foreman calling at cottages
rounding up his men

They walk on, laughing at their pedantry,
leaving a chargehand long gone,
a house in confusion.

Banjo

Skinny and twelve in Peg Leg's East End garden
where he swings his good leg a second after the
wooden one almost upright above parallel bars,
biceps taking the load

C major he shouts, *Move*. Then the end of his peg
kicks back and me angling my head to miss it.
His pendulum body slows, drops to his only foot,

points me inside to make some music while his
roaring *get on with it* attacks the room with its
gas mantles, and ashtrays strapped on armchairs

and I *every-good-boy* it, tune up with cloth ears, strum
awkwardly, thin voice humming *Goodnight Ladies*.
Back in its case I'm ready to walk home close to walls,

avoid other kids - learning music, like big words, sparks
the screech of hatespeak - crush my school cap into a pocket,
hear the creak of bars and now the scream of shells, wonder
if, rifle in hand, he huddled against trench sides.

Billy The Kid

Billy was the smartest kid around
at playing dead.

Blow a hole in his chest with a .45
and he'd hurtle six feet backwards
and lie perfectly still till his
mother called him in for tea.

Pierce his tank turret with a shell
and bits of him broke off
as it ricochetted around
until there was hardly any of him left.

Send him over the top and
he'd kill twenty Germans
before falling back in the mud
dying slowly and heroically.

Give him a mission impossible and
he'd return dragging the entire armada
before life oozed from him
lying face down on the beach.

And he could choke to death brilliantly
if you strangled him.

Dad's Dog

In the cafe with the others, pressing, squinteyed.
Gotta chance 'as it? Gonna win? Charlie, *Gets
out the traps quick, does it?* Wag sails in, fists
pumping, *'it that lid six, go on my son.*

Can hear Johnny, *Nah, she wouldn't let 'im
near 'er, pissed I fink.* Sits down next to me.
Finish in front, will it? Site agent in the corner
Man o' the moment, eh? they buyin' yer tea?

Sykesey's brother, *'ope it runs faster than
you cut in sashes.* Guffaws, heads back,
snared teeth, spittle. *Be of some fuckin' use
then, tell us.* Hear Billy at the counter, *Airship
on a cloud, luv.* Turns his head, *Romford, an' it?*

Come on, chrissake, 'orse's mouf an' that.
It's a dog, I say. *It can speak then. Can't
paint windows though.* Foreman rising. *Let's
do some, it's a big ceilin', long run till tea.*

They squeeze past him. Two strides back, face
into mine. *Better not cross that line in front if we
ain't on it.* Leave my babies on a raft to get cold.

Hit that lid is used when a greyhound leaves the traps very quickly and,
theoretically, its head will hit the inside of the rising gate. *Airship on a cloud*:
'sausage and mash'. *Babies on a raft*: 'beans on toast'.

Street Games

Flinging the ball at the pennies - tanners if you're flush -
on the paving slab against the end house wall, and mum
shouting down the street for your tea, and you run past

the parlour to the kitchen, stir the washing in the boiler
with the bleached broom handle while she salts greens,
squeal of fork inside a saucepan, hand wiping a brow;

and you want to run to the park, past the playground,
round the bandstand, on to the Flats, jump the stream
between houses, lean on a fluted lamppost and sate

yourself on mind flicks of skinny Iris at number two
or the misty silken space inside the thighs of principal
boys your dad takes you to see at Lyceum pantos,

but knowing you're only going out to the coins again
that no-one ever seems to hit.

Military Intelligence

Called him Buntah, did our washing, waved idiotically
as the truck took us to feed on rubber eggs and salt
tablets, for a Malayan dollar he'd tighten our beds
like drums, line up our flip-flops and straighten my
locker door pin-up so it smiled on the eighty of us

in a humid billet as we pulled on starched shirts
and spoon-buffed boots over woollen socks ready
to stand straight as wardrobes for an officer white as
flour to give nervous nods, and Buntah, in his strange
accent, said he would think of us when we guarded

the secret ammo dump and said hello to the passing
kids and took our rifles on up-country trains to guard
the arms we were taking to guard the arms we were
taking in futile tautology, and in the exercise when
Taffy shot blanks from six feet at a captain who'd

crossed the Straits with his men, surrounding us
while we were having a smoke, and in the Section
where we'd been getting *found in Jungle clearing one*
box of cornflakes six rounds of 202 one decapitated
head signals, and after I'd worked hours on a sketch

of a sniper, Buntah throwing it away thinking it
untidy, looking astonished when I yelled at him and
he sidled off, and in Yorkshire days later, ripping apart
army furniture to burn because it was Christmas,
no heat in the hut, and I already missed him
calling me *Jonnee Foreener.*

Laburnum Avenue

The sunray gate, garden steps, rockery either
side, the front door's leaded glass yacht, the
zigzag wallpaper, swallowing dry cake from

a Clarice Cliff plate, feet hardly touching the jade
and black carpet, a *don't ask don't get* nudge from
mum, tense with sister Joyce, easier with Con's

smokers cough and betting shop opposite, and
back to our tin bath, leather strapped ashtrays,
parlour's antimacassar homage to respectability;

walking the city now, still seeing curved bays,
herringbone bricks, Court foyers and chrome,
chevrons and pantiles and, somehow, smiling

auntie Joyce, her bright lipstick, tilted hat,
green fox fur, the glance down at me, that
look in her eyes, the recognition.

Bombsite

Found a wooden leg he kept throwing
in the air, brassiere full of rubble he swung
around his head, filled a bag with shrapnel
carried round for days.

'Alfie Herd did a turd behind the kitchen door
cat came up, licked it up, asked for 'apporth more.'

Tall-funnelled ships docked at terrace ends,
streets like giant gangways,
the blast absorbed, still floating,
rocking slowly.

Smashed houses in fake perspective like
a monochrome stage set, neat garden,
pipe smoker leaning on a roller-coaster
fence nodding in sympathetic circularity
with a cardigan'd neighbour

Patterned paper walls, dado rails, fireplaces
standing atop each other - an art installation
in a wasteland,
little Alfie swinging his bra,
ready for Goliath.

Aunt Rose's Funeral

The copy of *Saga* on a sill in the chapel,
plate glass views of pylons, your greying
cousins, the Benfleet bungalow, the pampas

grass she would pick to spray with lacquer
for the vase, the disappointments, George
not understanding ethnomethodological

phenomenology, Ernie suddenly seeming
likeable, the surprises, Bill the shop steward's
reluctant Marxism, a granddaughter's mini

skirt and high heels, the clichés, *nice spread
Vera, she 'ad a good innin's, lovely service,*
and centre circle, Stan nodding, joking, and

you can't join in, and the screaming
imperative to intellectualize, and still
hearing her calling you *Kenny.*

Different now

I'll have no truck said the trucker
with truckabilia.
No pagethrees and Fifties pics
of scantyclad Swedish beauties
(the only Nord Babe I want
is this Scania FLZ 18 DIESEL
eightygrandsworth of ABS,
syncromesh, kitchen sink, the lot).

The old 'uns 'll tell yer about it;
the birds, that 'ride for a ride' stuff,
the caffs, heartattacksonaplate.
Family man meself. Snaps of me kids
in me cab and 'er indoors on the door.
I'm professional. HGV'd. I don't get
up cars' arses. Intimidate. Mate.

Anyway, hop in luv. Hope those tight
jeans are clean, don't dirty me seat.
Right, here we go. Smooth innit?
D'you like it smooth? Hardly know
we're movin'. I move well. Know what
I mean? You got buttons or a zip…
Oh, come *on*! You stood there with -

Keep *still*. I'm pullin' over.
Wanna do yer.
Gonna screw yer.
Lay yer.
Play yer.
Slay yer.

The Last Stroke

The ward was once a billet for men at the aerodrome
its Art Deco tower guiding aircraft into a black and white
film, and where it was filled with the smell of oil and fags
it's now urine struggled through in slow motion by nurses,

doctors, everything living. The sister says *sorry,* for no more
is he the man who never touched me in anger - never touched -
had carried me on mean shoulders calling me *son,* but never
my name, had played keeper for his regiment, hid behind trees

at the back of the school shouting, *dive at their feet!* as legs
like giant slugs marched towards my goal; in the days when
a Big Mac was a large raincoat the ball weighed more than me
and covered in grass and guilt I'd watch the big boys cackling

back up the pitch as I shamefully pushed a foot back into a boot.
Now he's strangely spread under a sheet, like a goalie, the ball
past him; in bits, like pieces of Spitfire scattered across a runway.

Acknowledgements

Acknowledgements are due to the editors of the following where some of these poems or versions of them have appeared: *Rialto, Magma, Smiths Knoll, African American Review, Miracles and Clockwork* anthology: *The Best of Other Poetry, South, Bellevue Literary Review, Seam, Orbis,* and others too numerous to list.

THE HIGH WINDOW

The following collections of poetry are also available directly from our
website:
https://thehighwindowpress.com/the-press/

A Slow Blues, New and Selected Poems by David Cooke
Paperback; 178 pp; 9781291722826. September 2015. £12/$18

'Cooke is a convincing and rewarding poet whose work deserves a wide readership.'
Peter Bennet, *Other Poetry*

Angles & Visions by Anthony Costello
Paperback; 100 pp; 9781291722826. March 2016. £10/$18

'Costello's poems contain some beautiful and highly musical lines that bespeak a love
of poetry and all it can bring.'
Nick Cooke, *Sentinel Literary Quarterly*

The Emigrant's Farewell by James W. Wood
Paperback; 42 pp; 9781326498863. June 2016. £6/$8

'James W. Wood's poetry couples a finely tuned ear with a remarkable mix of
passion, idealism and down-to-earth good sense.'
Andrew Philip, author of *The Ambulance Box*

Four American Poets edited by Anthony Costello
Paperback; 132 pp; 9781326587093. September 2016; £12/$18

'May the ocean that separates our poetries find more bridges like this anthology!'
Thomas Lux

Dust by Bethany W. Pope
Paperback; 46 pp; 9781326498863. December 2016. £6/$8

Pope's writing has an intensely visual quality. Her use of imagery is strong – often
unflinchingly so.'
Neil Fulwood, *Stride*

From Inside by Anthony Howell
Paperback; 104pp; 9781326741334. March 2017; £10/$18

'Howell has style to spare and is happily unclassifiable.'
Peter Porter, *The Observer*

The Edge of Seeing by John Duffy
Paperback; 112 pp; 9781326984267. June 2017; £10/$18

'The effect is dizzying, consolatory and moving.'
Julia Deakin

End Phrase by Mario Susko
Paperback; 94pp; 9781326801656. September 2018; £10/$18

'Mario Susko is a poet of rare seriousness.'
Fiona Sampson

Bloody, proud and murderous men, adulterers and enemies of God
by Steve Ely
Paperback; 152pp; 9781326984229. December 2017; £10/$18

''Ely's poetry is passionately political, positively partisan.'
Tribune

Bare Bones by Norton Hodges; £10/$16
Paperback; 84 pp; 9780244033750. March 2018; £10/$18

'Norton Hodges's phrase "the integrity of life" underpins this knowing, poignant and
entertaining collection.'
Robert Etty

Wounded Light by James Russell
Paperback; 110 pp; 9780244645335. March 2018; £10/$18

'His eye for vivid telling details mark James Russell as a true story-teller, *and* a true
poet.'
Lee Harwood

Bone Antler Stone by Tim Miller
Paperback; 92 pp; 9780244009595. June 2018; £10/$18

'Our prehistory now has its poet laureate. Tim Miller makes old stones and artefacts
sing with new life.'
Barry Cunliffe, Emeritus Professor of European Archaeology, University of Oxford

Wardrobe Blues for a Japanese Lady by Alan Price;
Paperback; 88pages; 9780244065980; £10/$18

'Alan Price's alert eye for ordinary, sometimes everyday and recognisable, sights is
unerring.'
Alan Brownjohn

Trodden Before by Patricia McCarthy
Paperback; 82 pages; 9781908527332; £10/$18

'Patricia McCarthy is a serious poet and a seriously good one'
John F. Deane